Journey of a Lifetime

A Believer's Guide to Following Jesus Christ all the Way Home

MICHAEL A. MILTON, PH.D.

Tanglewood Publishing

Journey of a Lifetime

by Michael A. Milton, Ph.D.

ISBN-13: 978-0-9852897-4-4

© 2013 by Michael A. Milton

Published by Tanglewood Publishing

All rights reserved

Printed in the USA.

The author grants exclusive rights for printing or reproduction of the work in any format or form including digital to the publisher, Tanglewood Publishing. To use any portion of this book, you must first obtain permission in writing from the publisher.

Tanglewood Publishing

Fortress Book Service

1607 Tanglewood Dr.

Clinton, MS 39056

601-924-5020

www.tanglewoodpublishing.org

Introduction

This book is written for you. You have recently been awakened by the Spirit of God to see your spiritual poverty and Jesus Christ's wealth. Or you may be someone else. You have turned to Him as the resurrected and reigning Lord and Savior of your life. It may be that you trusted in Christ Jesus as a little boy or a little girl. That was many years ago. In between the child-like faith of your confirmation or profession of faith or baptism and your awakening and recommitment today, there is a trail of broken promises, broken relationships, and broken dreams. Behold, the old is passed away and all things have become new. New days are the ruling motif in the Christian life. *The Son* truly is *the sun* of our lives forevermore.

He is the *Sun* of optimism for living and dying. He is *the sun of* new hope in an otherwise hopeless world. Jesus Christ is *the sun* that radiates a glorious new light that beams its way through the old clouds that brought shadows to living. The clouds are being pushed out by a fast-moving front of refreshing life. Christ is life. That life is now in you.

This book is for this new, refreshing day. It is *your* day. This book is about that new life. That new life is in you. This book is about that Christ. That Christ is filling your life and drawing you home.

He saved you in order to bring you back to the garden: to find your fulfillment in your vocation as His son or daughter in being His child and being a part of His redemptive work in the world. So, why stand ye gazing up into the heavens? It is time to begin your journey of following the One who saved you. I pray this guide is faithful to the One who will never leave you nor forsake you.

How grateful I am to the Publisher for helping to get this book into your hands. I long to sit beside you, in this book, and share my heart with you. I want to make the journey with you in some way. Of course, I can do that only in text. What you truly need is a community of believers in a local assembly. What you really need is another under-shepherd who is faithfully preaching the truth that transforms from God's Word, the Bible, and who is administering the life-giving Sacraments of the Church. I pray you find that home. Pray to the Lord right now to bring you into that fellowship. Ask the One who saved you to settle you into that place of worship and service. He who started the work will complete it (Philippians 1:6).

I am humbled and honored to be with you in some small way in this journey of a lifetime.

Michael A. Milton, Ph.D.

Teaching Pastor, *Truth that Transforms*

LORD OF THE PAST

MY TESTIMONY
*to the Saving Work and
Keeping Power of Jesus Christ*

The Heart of My Ministry

Imagine reading the Psalms of David without knowing the presence and power of God in David's own life. Imagine reading the Epistles of Paul without knowing the history of God's grace and mercy in Paul's life. Imagine reading Peter's bold declaration about "...a living hope through the resurrection of Jesus Christ from the dead..." (1 Peter 1:3) and yet being ignorant of the grace he received after his glaring sin.

The power of the message of these men is communicated to us in an even greater way because we realize that these men knew grace personally. They had encountered the life-changing power of Jesus Christ in their own lives. Their personal testimony really formed the very heart of their ministries.

I would prefer that people read my curriculum vitae with an awareness of the presence and power of Jesus Christ in my life. My ministry is more than degrees, credentials, and personal statistics. It is the story of my encounter with the resurrected Jesus Christ. It only makes sense when one knows the reality of Christ alive in me.

Here, then, is my testimony.

This is the heart of my ministry.

And let me introduce the heart of my ministry by reading the heart of God that beats in me out of His Word.

The most memorable Scripture verses are those which seem to speak timeless truth to every generation in just a few words.

The Lord is my shepherd; I shall not want. (Psalms 23:1).

For God so loved the world, that he gave his only Son, that whoever believes in Him should not perish but have eternal life. (John 3:16).

And we know that all things work together for good to those who love God, to those who are the called according to His purpose. (Romans 8:28, NKJV).

...and the verse before us:

being confident of this very thing, that He who has begun a good work in you will complete it until that day of Jesus Christ; (Philippians 1:6, NKJV).

In a church where I pastored, I saw a little boy coming out of Sunday School carrying a craft project that I will never forget. It was a piece of colored paper with road construction signs all over it and his picture in the middle. At the bottom in glitter, it read,

> Please be patient. God is not finished with me yet.

The passage before us is one of my favorite passages. In it St. Paul, that great encourager of the saints, begins his "letter of joy" in the Epistle to the Church at Philippi, by seeking to stir up confidence in a people who were feeling a little shaken about some problems in their church. They had given him a financial gift, and he in return gave them a gift: life changing spiritual food. In essence, he told them,

> Please be patient with yourselves. God is not finished with you yet.

I want to use this passage—Paul's words and the message of the Holy Spirit for you today—to encourage you in your problems.

A lady once came to me for counseling. She had just become a Christian but felt that her life had been lived so far from God that she could never "catch up." In fact, she told me, through many tears, "I will never have a Christian home. I can never hope to live a happy Christian life. I'm just too messed up."

I told her that God had started a great work in her and He would never let her go. In fact, He is at work, even now, in completing what He started. He is making something beautiful of her life.

She asked me, "How can you be sure?"

I told her this story.

The Power of God at Work in One Life

He was born of an aging alcoholic career naval officer and an uneducated half-breed Choctaw Indian from Mississippi. They had met in an alcoholic recovery program, and with nothing else in common but their pain, they conceived a child. Despite attempts by the mother to abort the child, the father's insistence won out. Amid rumor, scandal, confusion, and embarrassment, a little boy was born in New Orleans, Louisiana, in the late 1950s.

It was soon apparent that this union, begun in pain, would end in pain. The child only complicated an otherwise hopeless situation.

At first the mother kept the child, but after her alcoholism bred schizophrenia, she abandoned him while the father was out to sea. One family account reported that she once hid her son in a doghouse. Mercifully, he was located by police. Needing to return to the sea to earn a living, the father turned to his sister back home in rural eastern Louisiana. Having just lost her husband and with no children of her own, that sixty-five year old woman took the little fellow in. There on a little chicken farm in the tall piney woods of a Louisiana-Mississippi border county, the old widow woman and the little boy began their new life together.

The first few years were difficult for the lad. His mother took him away several times, usually beating him with the buckle end of a belt until he bled. For years, the child would have nightmares of those beatings. Finally, the courts made him a ward of his aunt, and he would not know his biological mother again until years later.

When he was only six, the boy saw his father, having been discharged from active duty because of medical problems related to his alcoholism, accept an invitation from the aunt to go to church, just up the gravel road from where they lived. The three of them—the alcoholic father, his widowed sister, and the little boy—walked toward the country church. That Wednesday night, no sooner than the plumber-by-day-lay-preacher-by night began to open up the Scriptures in his sermon, the little boy watched his father kneel in the sawdust of that rough-hewn "tabernacle." He witnessed his daddy weeping in repentance and faith and saw the lay-preacher come down from the piney pulpit and lay his hands upon the head of the weeping man. The boy's daddy confessed his sins and pleaded, through heaving tears, to Jesus Christ to forgive him and save his soul. Within a few months, his father, sober and living for Christ, would fall victim to the years of abuse upon his body. That little boy would never forget the cold spring rain falling upon the steel gray casket of his new Christian father as it was lowered into the ground at the Methodist church yard in Walker, Louisiana.

One year later, the boy made a public profession of faith in Christ. His aunt would never miss one day of reading the Bible to him and laying her hands upon him to pray. Jesus Christ was as close as a brother. Yet for all of her love and all the benefits of being in a Christian home, a recurring thought haunted the little boy: I am the child with no parents; I am a loser. He could not shake that thought.

In spite of that, for the lad it was a real "Huck Finn" existence in that backwoods country. Actually it was the poorest parish in the state of Louisiana, but life felt very rich—rivers to cross, fish to catch, cows to chase, and old dogs to love. As an only child in a rural back woods area, his imagination was fed by books about faraway places, drawing, and dreams of becoming a super hero.

By the age of six he had won a poetry competition put on by the local electric co-op. At seven he had won a prize in an art competition. He was also beginning to show signs of promise in athletics. By age twelve he was a baseball all-star, MVP for the little league, and MVP for Pee Wee football. Soon he would go to the state high school baseball championships as the youngest high school starter in the state of Louisiana.

As a fullback, he became the leading rusher in the district, and as early as the ninth grade, he was being scouted by major universities.

He was also active in 4-H Club. His 4-H calf won every contest; and he and the Hereford, Little Joe, traveled far and wide, taking home a sack full of blue ribbons.

However, there was a problem. He was becoming distant from the childhood relationship with the God of his aunt. Though still very active in church life, he began to remove himself from church friends, choosing rather to associate with those who challenged authority.

Soon, his interest in football and 4-H Club and drawing was replaced by an interest in music. He preferred the deep and dark folk strains of the late 1960s. He began to delve into a world of darkness: new philosophies, drinking, smoking, and roaming around at late hours of the night. He was somehow kept from drugs and jail, but new interests in abstract art and underground music, which so reflected his own confusion, soon possessed him like a demon from hell and sucked promise and potential and sound judgment from his young life. This increasingly confused and wayward young man, within only weeks of his seventeenth birthday and against the wishes of his dear old aunt and the little country church, he left on what would become a prodigal journey of unbelievable loss and pain. His aunt cried out a warning that his action would bring him the greatest pain in his life and would break him. She told him that one day he would have to come home, and when he did, it would be in brokenness. He thought he knew better, and he left.

Along the prodigal road there were experiences with most everything one could imagine short of drugs and jail. There was a union that seemed to be repeating his own birth story.

Three children were born in those prodigal years. All diagnosed as profoundly deaf, they became the center of the young man's world. But that, too, would one day be lost.

In a little Episcopal church in Morgan City, Louisiana, the young man, then in his early twenties, heard the words of Jesus Christ given in a morning prayer service. For him, it was the moment of awakening. Like the prodigal son in the far country who recognized his desperate plight, this prodigal son saw his sinful life flash before him. He began a deliberate journey back to the Father's home, which would take several more years. At that point he was awakened to his sin but still searching for home. There came a time in his life when his aunt's wise words found their meaning and he came home—broken and weeping and tired. She kept telling him, "Son, God's got a plan and it's going to be all right. Remember, He is not finished with you yet. What God starts God completes."

Slowly but surely the plan began to unfold. He met and, this time with the blessing of his aunt, he married a single mother of four and began to settle down. But the pain of the past haunted him. In fact, his entire life kept coming before him with all of its darkness and sorrow.

The new family joined a small church in a rural area outside of Baton Rouge, and the pastor asked the young man, now in his late twenties, to go to an Evangelism Explosion clinic to hear a pastor named D. James Kennedy. There he heard the gospel of Jesus Christ presented. For the first time, he actually understood what grace meant—that God in Christ had lived the life he could never live and had given Himself as an offering for his own sins. He understood that it was only though faith and not because of works that anyone was saved. He understood the reality of God's sovereign power. He rushed home to tell his wife, and in joy and awe and wonder they began together to study the doctrines of grace. The sovereignty of God, once a mysterious doctrine, became like medicine to his soul as he realized that the words of his aunt were, in fact, very scriptural when she had said that God had a plan. The Bible said that all things work together for good to those who love God, and that He who started the good work would complete it.

Within only a few days, this sinner-saved-by-grace would begin to share the gospel of Jesus Christ with others. Within two years, he was elected to be an elder at his church, and then, realizing that God has summoned him to a ministry of Word and Sacrament, he surrendered to the call to preach. The man left a long career in management, and the family pulled up stakes and went to seminary, where he finished with honors and won the award in theology and preaching. Following seminary, he was accepted into a Ph.D. program at the University of Wales to study theology. Simultaneously, he accepted a call to be a church planter and later became senior minister of that church. By the time he finished his Ph.D. and accepted a call to a seminary to train others, he had led the church into their first building, founded a radio ministry, and a new Christian school for the area.

As I concluded my story of God's work in one man's life, the young woman, who had come to me for counsel feeling that she would never "catch up," looked at me, waiting for me to tell her what she had now figured out for herself. I told her, "Yes...I am that man."

And What of the People in My Life?

In an interesting twist that only God could write into reality, the mother who had sought to abort me and who had tied me up and beat me when I was a child would later be converted to Christ on her deathbed through the witness of the one she once sought to abort. At her death shortly afterward, it was my privilege to preach her funeral.

In a wonderful act of mercy and grace, God would bless Mae and me with the birth of our son in 1994—John Michael Ellis Milton—named after my father and myself. Placed in our arms as an act of grace, John Michael became a sign of God's remarkable gift of love. As Mae would write in her letter to our first church, "I feel like God has kissed our family." It is always amazing to me that God would so bless us that others would seek us out to learn how to rear children and how to have a happy home. But He does, and that, too, is a testimony of God's goodness and His amazing grace.

And what of my aunt? Well, Aunt Eva lived to the age of ninety-eight near her "son," the preacher. She was a charter member of the church I planted, and before she passed quietly into Glory, she gave us the only earthly possession she could afford to give: her blessing and her charge. "I love you all. Keep up the good work." She fell asleep in Jesus singing songs of praise. She could see that the plan of God was at work in the life of that boy she had raised for Christ.

What happened to those precious children removed from me at such a young age? At the exact time of my aunt's death, God began to miraculously open the door to what man had long since closed. On the very day that I conducted my aunt's funeral, I was approached by a man I had not seen for thirty years. He told me, "I know where the children are." God's mighty Hand of Providence moved after that—without me lifting one finger—and it was not long until my wife took a photograph of my reunion with my oldest child in front of her dormitory in Washington DC. Later, a letter came from my next oldest child—just starting college and eager to see me. The reunion story is not yet finished, but suffice it to say that after years of prayer and hope in the God of our lives, He is writing another testimony to His grace and mercy and sovereign power.

I have looked upon Mae's children as my children in Christ. Their children are my grandchildren and I love them as I love my own flesh. I have walked Mae's daughters down the aisles, I have baptized our grandchildren, and have been blessed beyond deserving.

And I say with that little Sunday School boy,

>Please be patient. God is not finished with me yet.

I tell you this story, not out of a morbid need to air my messy past, or because I desire to draw your attention to my failures or to my accomplishments, but only for this reason:

...He who has begun a good work in you will complete it until the day of Jesus Christ; (Philippians 1:6, NKJV)

God began the work in my life when I trusted in Him so many years ago, and He will do the same for you. Perhaps your story has similarities to mine—or may be completely different. His Spirit would not stop seeking me out, and will do the same for you. He was there when I left the "far country" to come home to the God of my childhood. He took all of my pain and my mistakes and my sorrow and has—like the wonderful gospel song—made something beautiful of my life. He will do the same for you.

And what of that woman who came to me with her concern that she could never have a Christian family? I conducted a wedding for her and her Christian groom a year later. On the last day of my pastorate before accepting a call to lead a seminary, I baptized their little boy. As she looked up at me, I once again saw tears. But this time they were Philippians 1:6 tears. God was completing what He had started in her life.

(I understand that her life grew more complicated and has not been as tidy as this would make it sound. I would say to her now: God is not finished with you yet.)

Let me give you three truths from God's Word in Philippians 1:6 that will change your life:

1. *First, this passage teaches that God must begin the work—not you.*

It is not until you learn and yield to the old Reformed doctrine of God's grace alone that you can enjoy eternal life and assurance of it. Are you perhaps trusting in your works? For years I trusted in the faith of my aunt without understanding it myself, and it cost me dearly. Could there be someone reading this who can never look back to a time when you recognized that Christ did it all and that you are absolutely dependent upon Christ alone for works of righteousness and forgiveness of sins? If you are that person, then do away with your own religion now and turn to the faith taught in God's Word. Do it now. Turn to Jesus Christ and cry out to Him alone. Throw your works as far from you as you can. They will bring you nothing but sorrow in this life and eternal sorrow in the life to come. To know Christ and to trust in Him alone is to know the joy of all joys. The invitation is before you.

2. *Second, it is comforting to note that God begins the work of salvation "in you"—that is, God works through ordinary sinful and broken folks who turn to Him in repentance and faith.*

Whatever it is that you have done, He can forgive you and use you in some way. God's grace and mercy are greater than your worst sins. He may not use you as a pastor or teacher, but He will always use you as a witness to His grace. God begins His greatest work in those most greatly crushed. His power is demonstrated in your weakness. I ask you to offer your pain and your heartaches to the only One who can make sense of it. God works through people like you.

3. *Third, this passage teaches that God will complete it. God will see you through your every trial.*

What a great consolation to the life of one who is going through what one ancient writer has called "The Dark Night of the Soul." What an encouraging doctrine for all who have fallen so deeply into sin that they would have otherwise lost all hopes of new life.

This text in Philippians—one of so many—points to the single greatest liberating truth in all of Scripture: the sovereignty of God.

What Does All of This Mean?
How Does Philippians 1:6 Work in Your Life?

There was once a lumberjack who took his little son with him into the woods for the day. While there, a great storm came up, and the creeks in the woods began to flood. The two were practically trapped between the woods and their home by a swift-moving creek that was rising by the minute. At the bank of that creek the dad took his little son into his arms and held him tightly. The little boy, out of sheer exhaustion, fell asleep on his father's shoulder.

The next thing the boy knew, he was awakened to see the morning sun flooding through the curtains in his room. He was in his own bed, clean, dry, and safe. His father was leaning on the doorway with a mug of coffee in his hand. He was giving the boy his usual first smile of the day.

You see, God's sovereignty is like that. When, in the storms of life, it seems that the problems of life begin to rise so fast that we could never get home again, we can rest in our all-powerful Father. God will carry us through the worst of storms all the way home.

God began the work in my life, and in the midst of the storms, I finally leaned to trust in His sovereign power.

You can do that too, right now. And you will one day wake up to see that He brought you safely all the way home.

His promises bring abundant life here and now and eternal life with God when we die.

I invite you who would commit your life to Jesus Christ alone for eternal life and those who would re-commit to trusting in the sovereignty of God to join me as I pray:

> Lord of life, we thank You that You have the sovereign power to pick up broken lives and turn them into trophies of grace. We here offer You our lives. We confess that Christ lived the life we can never live and that His death paid the penalty for our sins and that His rising again from the dead secured our eternal life. Forgive us for unbelief and work a work of grace in our lives.
>
> Lord of life, use us to tell others and to encourage others who need healing.
>
> In the Name of Jesus Christ our Lord, we pray. Amen.

LORD OF THE JOURNEY

The Journey of a Lifetime

Have you trusted in the resurrected and living Christ?[1] Then God has revealed to you that according to His Word, the Holy Scriptures,[2] your faith is a gift of God,[3] not earned or deserved, and freely bestowed upon you by the Lord of life.[4] Your faith comes as you perceive your situation—a most hopeless condition—that you, like all of us, are separated from God in our sins,[5] in the progeny of Adam,[6] and in need of a Savior to live the life we cannot live and die the atoning death that should be ours.[7] That Savior is Jesus of Nazareth.[8] He is fully God and full Man.[9] He came to die on the cross for our sins, and to rise again for our new life.[10] In a word, Jesus is God.[11] He is the fullness of the triune God in bodily form.[12] He came of miraculous birth.[13] He performed miracles[14] and his powers over life and death, over the wind and the waves, validated His own self-identity.[15] He was crucified for our sins. He rose from the dead on the third day, was seen in His resurrected state by over five hundred men at one time, and He ascended into heaven where He is seated ever interceding for those who will believe and who have believed in Him. He is coming again in glory. The faith summed up in the Apostles' Creed and the Nicene Creed, as well as historic Christian statements of faith such as the Westminster Confession of Faith and the Larger and Shorter Catechisms is the faith of the Bible. To receive this Christ by faith is to receive everlasting life and abundant life here and now.

Yet faith in Jesus Christ is the beginning of, literally, the journey of a lifetime.

Peter, one of the disciples, who was also an apostle, came to believe in Jesus as the Christ (or Messiah, Anointed One, and Promised One of God). He taught that Jesus came to deliver us from our sins through His perfect life and atonement, and that Christians must *grow in the grace and knowledge of Jesus Christ.*

> *But grow in the grace and knowledge of our Lord and Savior Jesus Christ. To him be the glory both now and to the day of eternity. Amen.*
> *(2 Peter 3:18)*[17]

This does not happen in one sermon, one reading, or one class. It is a lifetime of following the Lord in the three major ways that Peter outlines here.

Growing in Grace

As a new believer, you need to know, as we all should, that we were saved by grace. We were not saved by what we "brought to the table," but what Christ did. Period. Christ plus nothing.[18] "G-R-A-C-E: God's riches at Christ's expense" as Dr. D. James Kennedy used to say.[19] We are saved by this "great exchange" of Christ's life lived for us (a perfect life which God requires in His Law) and His atoning death on the Cross (the verdict of sin is death and Christ died for you so that you could live with Him forever).[20] He got your sin. You get His life. That is the divine plan of salvation in Christ Jesus our Lord.[21] That is grace. But what is it to grow in grace?

To grow in grace is to grow in thanksgiving to God for His grace. To grow in grace is to recognize that God is due all of the glory for our lives. To grow in grace is to move closer to Him in every way, not in a relationship of earning His favor through our works, but in worshipping Him and enjoying Him forever for His love, mercy, presence and power all showered on us through His Holy Spirit. To grow in grace is also to grow together in grace. To grow in grace is to grow into a place of spontaneous, doxological combustion, "to God alone be glory!" That is the importance of Peter's statement here. He was writing to the Church, not just to one believer. We grow in grace through the ordinary means of grace offered to us through God in His Church, the supernatural Body of Believers that He has adopted into His forever family. More about those "means" or "ways to access" God's grace in a moment.

Grow in grace throughout all of your life. Come to love Christ more and more for His sovereign grace, His divine activities on your behalf, and you will come to live a life that is free, peaceable, and just. You will also begin to surely show that grace to others. You can become as patient with others as God is patient with you. Grace, like all of God's truths, has practical everyday importance. Think of how the world would look if more and more people grew in this grace. Well, we don't have to dream. Grace is on its way as the Kingdom of Jesus Christ continues to grow, one person at a time, just like you.[22] Families, nations and the whole world will be impacted by His grace.[23]

A journey of a lifetime begins with grace.[24] But grace, as the way that Christ saves us, and keeps us, and leads us all the way home to Him one day, is strengthened by another way that we as believers must grow.[25]

Growing in Knowledge

You must know that we are not saved by just having knowledge of the plan of salvation, knowledge of Jesus Christ and His identity as God in the Flesh, or knowledge that God is One yet exists in three Persons: the Father, the Son and the Holy Spirit. You are not saved by *only* knowledge, yet to be saved you must receive those basic truths.[26] You must hear the Gospel that contains truths—like grace[27]— which form cogent ideas, or divine revelation from God communicated to us by the Bible.[28] Knowledge of God's Revelation of Himself in the Bible is necessary to believe. Yet knowledge of God's Word, the Bible, which was written by God's Spirit through prophets and apostles and teachers across thousands of years and in 66 different books, is united in what has been called a "scarlet thread of redemption," the covenant of grace.[29] God created all that is. Mankind fell into sin. And for the rest of what we call the Bible, God makes a sacred pledge, a "covenant," that He will provide what He requires through His Messiah, who is Jesus our Lord. The Bible is thus about that promise, about the people who were used to bring that promise to fruition, and about God's dealings with us. For this reason we should continue to grow in knowledge of God and of His Word.

If we do not, we will grow weak and spiritually malnourished. This can lead to spiritual diseases of the soul and to temptations from the enemy, Satan (a fallen angel who presently is allowed by God to exist, with his demons, other fallen angels, and who, having opposed Jesus and lost, now "goes about like a roaring lion seeking whom he may devour"). It can also lead to bad decisions, lack of wisdom, and being deprived of the fellowship of other believers who are also on the journey of a lifetime. Failing to grow in knowledge of God and His Word can lead to danger, for while we cannot lose what God has won, to willfully ignore God's Word, should rightfully lead us to question whether we truly believed unto eternal life, or whether we believed as a sort of experience that fizzled out like a flat Coke.

God wants us to be strong for the journey of a lifetime and that means growing in knowledge of Him. God wants you to be familiar with your own family history as it were. He wants you to know the names of those who have gone before. He has given us stories to relate to our own story and to the larger Story of His love in Jesus our Savior. He has given us knowledge that leads to self-knowledge also. In the Bible we see a mirror that shows us ourselves, as well as shows us God. To grow in understanding of this knowledge is to desire to grow closer to God. It is not just knowledge for knowledge's sake! It is for, literally, *God's sake* (that is, for His glory)—and for your sake. And that leads me to the third great truth in 2 Peter 3:18.

Growing in Christ

We grow in grace and knowledge in a Person, the Lord Jesus Christ. Christianity is not just an idea. Christianity is not just a religion without a relationship. Christianity is centered in *the Person* of the God-Man, our Friend, our Redeemer, our Mediator between man and God, our Hope, our Sovereign, and our Lord and Savior, Jesus of Nazareth. He was prophesied in the Old Testament over three hundred times.[30] He was born, according to the Scriptures and in fulfillment of ancient prophecy, in Bethlehem of Judea, to a virgin named Mary. Her husband, Joseph, did not lie with his wife until after Jesus was born (other children were born to them later as the New Testament shows). Joseph was a good man, a man chosen by God, as revealed by an angel, to rear this child, and give Jesus his home, lineage, and name. Joseph was the adoptive father of Jesus and that fact forever seals the beauty of adoption.[31] You and I are adopted into God's family. The world sometimes looks down on covenants and promises and vows, like adoption, as something less than physical inheritance. Not so in the Bible. *In the Bible, covenant and promise are more powerful than DNA.* You are saved by grace, through the knowledge of your sin and need of a Savior, Jesus Christ. You become God's child and He will never let you go.[32] When you die, your soul goes immediately to be with Christ though your remains stay here until the great resurrection, when Jesus comes again. Yet the One who made all of that possible was Jesus Himself. We grow in grace and in knowledge, but that growth is focused on *a Person, Jesus.*

If we love someone we want to spend time with that one. So, too, if you love Jesus you will want to spend time with Him. How? This leads me to now focus on the biblical answer to how Christians in Peter's day and Christians in our day are to grow in the grace and knowledge of Jesus Christ. We are to do so through the "means," or "ways" that God has appointed. These are supernatural. They provide a heaven-sent power that gives us strength for our journey of a lifetime.

The Means of Grace

When we look into God's revelation of Himself in the Bible, we learn that there are three main ways or "ordinary means" by which a new believer (or any believer, for that matter) grows in this journey called discipleship as a follower of Christ. They include Word, Sacrament, and Prayer.

Word

We grow in the grace and knowledge of Jesus Christ through His Word, the Bible.[33] You cannot be a believer and grow without God's Word. To grow in the Bible is to be a member of a body of believers where the Word of God is regularly taught, revered as inerrant (without error) and infallible (divine and thus incapable of ever being wrong or giving wrong counsel). That Word should be read by you personally as you grow by reading your own Bible each day. The Bible says in Psalms One that the one who does this is like a strong tree that is planted by a river of life-giving water. You will grow in the grace and knowledge of God if you grow in the Bible through reading its sacred contents, not only privately, but within the community of others, as a member of a Bible believing congregation, and through singing the Word, hearing the Word preached, and through reading the Word to your family daily. (We call that "family worship" and I always say that I would want our church to be a "home" and our home to be a "church" in the sense that God's Word is taught there.) It is impossible to grow in the grace and knowledge of Jesus Christ without growing in God's Word.

We should also be ready to share that Word with others. It is not just pastors who share the Word. Every believer is called upon to share the Word. To do so means that we know the Word ourselves. Even giving a testimony of what God has done for you, and knowing the Word and how the Word frames and explains our sin, our salvation, and our hope in Christ is essential to "getting it right" in telling the Gospel story to others. There is no greater joy than sharing the Word of Christ with another. Since God's Word has supernatural power and divine promises attending it, we can be sure that His Word will accomplish all that He intends. Share Christ in His Word and leave the results to Him. Funny thing though, the more we share that

Word, the more others believe.

So having a Bible, reading it, listening to it as it is faithfully preached, gathering with others under that authority and teaching of the Word in a faithful assembly or local church, is absolutely critical and necessary for growth.

Sacrament

A "Sacrament" is an old word, which means a "sign."[34] The Lord God left us two visible signs that help us on our journey of a lifetime: baptism and the Lord's Supper (at times called communion, in the Bible, or the Eucharist, meaning "thanksgiving'). As Christ our King governs His subjects spiritually through the Church (not a building or an organization, but the called out pastors and elders, deacons and members of an assembly recognized by other believers as genuine), so too, these Sacraments are dispensed for our growth through the Church.

If you have never been baptized, then the Lord commands that you should be. Talk to your pastor. Talk to him about your desire to follow Jesus Christ. Meet with him to discuss baptism. While some in the Body of Christ differ on the method and candidates for baptism, it seems clear that baptism is for believers and their children.[35] Baptism does not save. Baptism is a pouring of water to represent an entrance into the Kingdom of God, to mark out those, like babies, who are children of believers, and who have the benefits of godly parents who will rear them in the grace and knowledge of Christ until they stand on their own to make their own confession of faith. Baptism is also a sign and a seal (God's own kingly insignia) to represent the shedding of blood and washing of a person to be clean before God. Baptism is not something we do for God. Baptism is a gift of God to us. It is His sign, His testimony, not ours. If you have not been baptized, be obedient to Christ and go quickly to your pastor and schedule a time of baptism based on your profession of faith. Later, as you observe others being baptized, you are called upon to recollect how you were saved; how, perhaps, God revealed Himself to you through a preacher's sermon, through a friend's witness, through an author's words, or how God gave you to Christian parents who taught you the Gospel from the time you can remember anything at all. No matter how He reached you, baptism calls each of us to reaffirm our faith that we have been cleansed from sin by the shedding of the blood of Jesus. *You are reminded that you are a member of His family, not because of what you did, but what He did for you.*

The other Sacrament, or sign and seal of God's plan of salvation, is the Lord's Supper. In this Sacrament there are two elements that God uses to signify His love: the bread and the cup. In the bread and the cup, which Jesus instituted in the Last Supper, we are given a Sacrament, not for entrance, but for lifelong nourishment. When Jesus gave the bread and the cup at the last supper with His disciples, He told them— and us—that the bread is His body given for us. The cup is His blood shed for us. The sacrament is a sign and seal, and is for believers. It is to be received through Christ's Body, the Church. The Lord's Supper demands that we remember the death of Jesus for our sins. The Lord's Supper recalibrates our faith upon that central act of redemption, liberating us from the auction block of sin, by looking again at the cross of Christ. By doing so, we are drawn closer to Jesus, closer to each other, and even closer to those who have gone before and those who believe around the world. In this, it is Communion. In that it is God's plan of salvation, following the ancient Passover of the Old Testament, it is our "Eucharist," our "great thanksgiving." Thus the Lord Supper has a sense of awe, wonder, mystery, beauty, gratitude, and Holy Communion with God and each other. As often as the Church offers Communion, it is your obligation to be there. For in it you grow. You grow, as Peter said, in the grace and knowledge of Jesus Christ.

These Sacraments strengthen us for the journey of a lifetime.

Prayer

Ole Hallesby, a Norwegian pastor-scholar wrote a book in 1931 entitled, simply, *Prayer*.[37] In that book Hallesby wrote,

> "To pray is to let Jesus come into our hearts."[38]

I believe that there is Biblical genius in his brevity. Speaking to God as we read His Word, hear His Word, and are drawn back again and again to His plan of salvation in the Sacraments, is called prayer, and through this, Christ communes with us. We cannot grow in grace or knowledge of Jesus without prayer.

Prayer is coming to God silently or vocally, sometimes with only a groaning that cannot be uttered (because our great burden overwhelms us), with our petitions, our afflictions, our joys, our dreams and hopes for justice, our prayers for others, for the Gospel itself to go forward, for family, for authority, the sick and needy, ourselves, and, especially, with worship towards God. In prayer many believers often say that we use A-C-T-S as an acronym for approaching Him: we *adore* Him in praise, we *confess* our sins before Him, we *thank* Him, and we bring *supplications*—our pleas and requests—to Him for others and for ourselves. We pray kneeling, standing, sitting, lying prostrate before Him, in private, in public, daily, momentarily, at certain hours of the day, and, as Paul said, "without ceasing"—that is, the "connection" between God and His creature is never to be broken. Don't hang up on God when you say "Amen." True prayer never really concludes.

The Lord's Prayer[39] is known to many. "Our Father who art in heaven, hallowed be Thy name…" (Matt. 6:9 RSV) But it could also be called The Disciples' Prayer. For Jesus was responding to a request by a disciple to be taught how to pray. Thus, we pray to Our Father, not *my* Father, but *our* Father. Our faith and our growth in Christ always happens in the context of the

Church. We should be in an assembly of God's people together, a local church, that is part of that one true universal Church. ("Catholic" is the older word here, meaning not just universal, but orthodox and holding to the basics of our faith stated, for instance, in the Apostles' Creed [which we have provided for you at the end of this document]). And from there, each of the petitions teaches us how to approach the Lord: to remember His glory in heaven, that we are to hallow His very name, that we are to pray for the coming of His kingdom in our lives and in the lives of others and in the world, that we should be grateful and relate to God in total dependence upon Him for our daily needs, that we should be penitent before the Lord, mindful that we are sinners saved by grace and coming not on our merits but through the merits of our Lord and Savior Jesus Christ, that we should be forgiving others as the Father forgave us, through Jesus Christ, that we are weak and in need of His guiding us out of temptation's way and into the way of goodness, and that all of these things are brought under His Lordship as King.

Others have simply put it this way: a disciple must be marked by a love of the Bible, worship, prayer, fellowship, and witness. These are the ways, the "means of grace," in which we are strengthened for the journey.

Years ago, I thought I could go it alone. I thought that I had enough knowledge of God to make it to Heaven. But I was shown, in the Bible and in my own soul as the Holy Spirit came to me, personally, that I was depending on self and not the Savior, Jesus. I needed to come to Him by receiving His free gift of eternal life by grace through faith. When I did, my life was changed.[40] And now, maybe yours is as well. You are on a journey and it is, indeed, a journey that winds its way through all of the seasons of our lives. We don't get there all at once, unless we are taken home to be with him. In this life, we grow in the grace and knowledge of Jesus Christ as a day in and day out, week in and week out, year in and year out way of life. We grow through

Word, Sacrament and Prayer. But soon we will be Home. And then we will look back to see that He who called us was the same One who sustained us, preserved us, and through all circumstances—good and bad—was with us all the way. And we will come into His very presence and be able to say,

"Truly, Lord, thanks to You, this was a journey of a lifetime."

LORD OF THE MISSION

Called to be Taught;
Taught to be Sent

What Makes Christianity Different?

The Gospel of Mark is written to people trying to figure out what makes Christianity different. Who is Jesus? And what does it mean to be His disciple in this world?

Mark answers those questions in His Gospel. He often does it not only with the Word but even with the way He presents the Word. In Mark 6, for example, Mark shows how Jesus Christ answers the question, "What does it mean to be a disciple of Jesus in the world today." The way he does it is simply amazing. He panels stories side by side, overlapping, interweaving, until the careful student begins to see that the answer is hitting him over and over again. In this case, before Mark tells the story about Jesus sending out the Twelve, He tells the story of Jesus' rejection at Nazareth. Then, after he starts the sending story, he sandwiches that story in between the story of the beheading of John the Baptist. Rejection to sending to martyrdom. The net effect is to powerfully press home the meaning of discipleship in the world.

And now we come to the meat in between the bread. Will you give attention to God's Word?

> *And he called the twelve and began to send them out two by two, and gave them authority over the unclean spirits. He charged them to take nothing for their journey except a staff—no bread, no bag, no money in their belts— but to wear sandals and not put on two tunics. And he said to them, "Whenever you enter a house, stay there until you depart from there. And if any place will not receive you and they will not listen to you, when you leave, shake off the dust that is on your feet as a testimony against them." So they went out and proclaimed that people should repent. And they cast out many demons and anointed with oil many who were sick and healed them. (Mark 6:7-13)*

What is a True Disciple?

I was moving closer to a PhD. and further from God and I was a pastor. And I think what happened to me can happen to any of us.

I told you earlier about the details leading to my grace awakening and the new birth it brought in my life. I have related about my call to preach. But I have not told you why I wanted to immediately do research work in theology after seminary. I believe then and now that God had called me to seek further study when I heard the words of James Montgomery Boice to pastors, that the pulpit was deserving of the finest training and study, that it was as important to prepare yourself for the work of the pulpit and parish as it was to do so for the seminary. I wanted to fine tune my mind, learn the tools of research, and discipline myself for the work of study and preaching. So, with a heart for study and a heart for missions, I simultaneously became a church planter and a Ph.D. student. I don't recommend it. It aged me considerably. But somewhere along the way, I think I began to lose my vision. I lost sight of the goal of the study and became immersed in the work as if the research was the goal. That is when God sent me to get fixed at the manse of a Welsh preacher named Mr. Cox. My wife and I joined Mr. Cox, the pastor of Bethel Congregation in Gorseinson, Wales, for tea after evening worship. Now Mr. Cox was a very dramatic Welsh preacher who would fall on his knees during the service and shake the Communion rail as he literally wept for souls to repent. He would often call out people by their name, as he did with me one time to my astonishment, and use live examples of what Christ could do in a person's life. Like any respectable Welsh preacher, he carried a flowing handkerchief that cascaded out of his suit pocket and he came complete with a Dylan Thomas lock of hair that fell down over his eyes, so that as he stretched out his right hand to make a point in his sermon, he could deftly use his other hand to throw the lock back over his scalp. It was an ingenious move, very theatrical and yet one got the impression that this was just Mr. Cox and not one bit of acting.

Well, as I say, we went to his manse on Alexander Street in that quaint little working class village to have tea. After some serious conversation about theological matters, he looked at me and said, "Mr. Milton, you really are a studied man, aren't you? I mean all of this study here and in that doctoral program there with those learned men at the University and all. I mean, Mr. Milton, you really are something!" What could I say? The devil was blinding me and he knew it.

"Now, Mr. Milton, I suspect that you would like to go to my study to see all of my books, wouldn't you?" "Oh, yes!" I said like a kid on Christmas morning and I jumped up ready to go. "Alright, then," he popped up, "Let's have a look at my great library." I followed him up the old staircase in the manse and we arrived at the top and went into the room he called his study. It was dark, but I could see one thing: shelf after shelf after shelf was empty. I was confused.

"Well, what do you think of my fine library, Mr. Milton. Do you think the boys at the University would approve?" I stood speechless, awaiting the show to carry on. "Well, Mr. Milton, there on that table, there are all of my books! All 66 of my books!" There, in the midst of an empty library was a table with a Bible on it. Nothing else. In fact, no other furnishings in the room save a chair. All I could do was smile. "Now, look here, Mr. Milton," the preacher said, as he looked me in the eye. "God told me that I was depending too much on books and not enough on His Book. So I got rid of them all!" I secretly wished he had thought of me when he was donating his library to others, but I said nothing. "Mr. Milton, you must never allow anything to get in the way of trusting in the Holy Spirit and His Word alone." And I felt then as I feel now, that God spoke to me that night in that manse in Wales and reminded me: I am called to be taught and I am taught to be sent.

It is possible for people to think that they are Christians, but to miss it. For this is a Christian: Called, Taught and Sent. And moreover it is possible for even true believers in Jesus Christ to get confused about this essential character of the Christian faith.

The Gospel of Mark is here to help clarify and I pray God uses this message to bring us back to the basics of this message in Mark 6:7-13.

The sending of the twelve in Mark is, not surprisingly, the shortest of this account, which appears also in Matthew and in Luke. It is in Matthew's account that we have the testimony of the tremendous teaching about what it is to be a disciple. It is in Matthew's expanded story of the sending of the Twelve that we have such teaching as:

"The student is not above His teacher" (Matthew 10:24 NIV);

"If the head of the house has been called Beelzebub, how much more the member of his household!" (Matthew 10:25b NIV)

"Do not be afraid of those who kill the body but cannot kill the soul. Rather be afraid of the One who can destroy both soul and body in hell." (Matthew 10:28 NIV)

"Whoever acknowledges me before others, I will also acknowledge before my Father in heaven. But whoever disowns me before others, I will disown before my Father in heaven." (Matthew 10:32 NIV)

"Do not suppose that I have come to bring peace to the earth. I did not come to bring peace, but a sword." (Matthew 10:34 NIV)

Anyone who loves his father or mother more than me is not worthy of me; anyone who loves his son or daughter more than me is not worthy of my and anyone who does not take his cross and follow me in not worthy of me. Whoever finds his life will lose it, and whoever loses his life for my sake will find it." (Matthew 10:37-39NIV)

That last verse bore down into my soul in a morning prayer service in a little Episcopal church in Morgan City, Louisiana, while I was on a sales call for Dow Chemical. It led me to see the shallowness of my profession and started me on a journey that eventually led me face to face with my sinful soul and my only salvation in Jesus Christ.

This is the context. Mark is giving us the account of the sending of the twelve, sandwiched between rejection at Nazareth and the beheading of John. In this we come to see what it means to be a Christian.

We are called to be taught and taught to be sent. Now I want to briefly consider the fact that a true believer must be called and taught, and then I want to draw a little more from this passage as we see Jesus' teaching about being sent.

First, we need to make sure we understand that a true disciple of Jesus is called by Jesus.

Jesus called His disciples as they were working in their jobs. Here in this passage, before they are sent, He again calls them to Himself, the Bible says. Jesus calls us in salvation, He calls us in teaching, and He calls us in sending. The essential character of a disciple is not a person who turns over a new leaf, or makes a decision for Jesus, but whose life is radically transformed by an encounter with the Call of Jesus on his or her life.

This is the uniform teaching of the Word of God:

"You did not choose me, but I chose you and appointed you that you should go and bear fruit…" (John 15:16 ESV);

"The God of this people Israel chose our fathers…" (Acts 13:17 ESV)

"…He chose us in him before the foundation of the world, that we should be holy and blameless before him…" (Ephesians 1:4 ESV)

Now the issue is simply this: Jesus has come. His Word is in front of you and He is calling you. Dietrich Bonhoeffer put it better:

> "One thing is clear: we understand Christ only if we commit ourselves to Him in a stark 'either-or.' He did not go to the cross to ornament and embellish our life. If we wish to have him, then He demands the right to say something decisive about our entire life. We do not

understand Him if we arrange for Him only a small compartment of our spiritual life. Rather, we understand our spiritual life only if we then orientate it to Him alone or give a flat 'No.'"[41]

The question today is, "Is Jesus calling you?" You are here for a purpose and it is not to fill space in a church, or to have a nice church membership for your resume. It is either you have heard the compelling call of Christ on your life or it is nothing.

The essential character of discipleship is the call of God. It is the call of God in Christ in salvation. It is the call of God in Christ in discipleship also, for here we see that these men who were called to Christ were called to Christ again before they would be sent. We cannot live the Christian life without coming to Christ again and again and again. Not for salvation, mind you (that is a once and always thing) but for guidance, for direction and for clarification of our lives as His disciples.

Second, we need to make sure we understand that a true disciple of Jesus is taught by Jesus.

Again, I say that Matthew gives us more of the account of Jesus teaching just before they were sent, but Mark shows this in a different way. Mark shows us, dramatically, that Jesus taught them before they went out as His disciples through the example of His own life. Jesus was rejected. Mark doesn't record the actual teaching that went on, he just shows the Roman Christians in the story about Jesus' rejection right before the Twelve are sent. Mark often leaves it for his audience to fill in the blank. He moves quickly. But He doesn't miss it. They are called to be taught.

We have developed, it seems to me, in many circles an almost distaste for learning. It is as if to do serious study of the Word of God, to inquire into the nature of God and into that which is properly called "theology" or the study of God, somehow leaves us suspect. I recognize that much of this suspicion of learning and faith comes from perfectly faithful men going off to seminary to become godless liberals. But must we again throw the baby out with the bathwater? Mark Noll of Wheaton College wrote an outstanding book on this very subject, which he called: *The Scandal of the Evangelical Mind*. Noll began his first page with this statement:

> *"The scandal of the evangelical mind is that there is no evangelical mind."*

Now that is hyperbolic and disturbing, to draw you into the book. But his premise is that we have failed to "renew our minds" as Paul called us to do. We have failed to love God with our minds as Jesus called us to do. We may have forgotten that the Great Commission is to go and "teach them whatsoever I have commanded you." You are not ready to be sent until you are being taught by Jesus. And I don't mean, on the other hand, a sterile, academic teaching, but a sit-at-the-feet-of-the-Savior academy. As a result, we have been satisfied with the hem of Christ for salvation, but have missed his deeper teaching for life transformation. But Jesus taught his disciples. As a result, some of us have reproduced a Christianity that does not contain the whole counsel of God and may not even be true faith. To be a disciple is to sit at the feet of the Master.

Are you going to be seated at the feet of the Master? In His Word? In authentic, soul-changing, heaven-pleading, Christ-saturated prayer?

Third, we need to make sure we understand that a true disciple of Jesus is sent by Jesus.

Now we need to see this as we move on. We need to see that the teaching didn't stop when they were sent. Indeed, they knew very little. The sending was a part of the teaching. For you see, you cannot be a disciple without being called by Jesus, taught by Jesus, but also sent by Jesus. Jesus sends these out and it is now that I want us to consider the three characteristics of this sending.

True believers, like the Twelve, are sent with a Commission.

The commission here is simple.

Go.

You must go. They were not called and taught to grow spiritually fat and sluggish but to go and bear fruit. True believers are people who are reproducing their faith, teaching the teachings of their Savior to others.

Go Together.

They are sent out two-by-two. This accords with all of the teaching of God in the Bible, for testimony is established in twos. Thus, you have Peter and John, Paul and Barnabas, Paul and Silas and so forth.

I once had another minister tell me, "I will give you a secret to the pastorate. 'Never do ministry alone.'" I have not forgotten that. Pastors equip others. My work is to equip the saints for the work of ministry and I do that in the company of others.

In the Army, we have something that is known as the buddy system. And I think this is what Jesus is doing. You go into battle with a battle buddy. He looks out for you, he covers your back, he gives you encouragement, he holds you accountable, he sees what you see and together you make better decisions.

My beloved brethren, there is a great principle here and that is that God has placed us in a team called the Church. There are to be no lone wolves in the Church. In Acts 2, after the great outpouring of the Spirit at Pentecost, we immediately see the saints gathered into local assemblies. Indeed, the very word "church" in the Bible is "ecclesia," and it means "the assembly." In the Old Testament that word is "Qara" and it is translated "Congregation." In Hebrews, the word "congregation" is rendered "Church." That is right. It is the same thing. The people of God are not to "forsake the assembling of themselves together." They are to *have church*, literally in the Greek. To assemble is to church. There are to be no loose cannons in the Body of Christ. Paul told Titus, "Set in order the things that remain, appoint elders in every city." That is plural: elders.

All that is to say that God intends for His people to be gathered together in local fellowships under the spiritual covering of pastors and elders. Some of you today are not there and need to find a place where you can be in a covenanted relationship with a local assembly. I encourage you to do ministry, to be sent out, with other believers somewhere. It is God's will.

Go with authority.

Jesus told these disciples that they had authority over demons. Now we need to always look at the Bible with redemptive-historical lens, otherwise we will forever be confused. This was a specific time in redemptive history. These twelve were sent directly Jesus. The word for sent in the Greek is the root from which we get the word *apostle*. There are no more apostles. But still every Christian is sent forth with an authority from Jesus. That authority is to proclaim what God has done for you. That is what the Man of the Tombs did. He was healed and delivered and told what things God had done for him. Peter says:

"But you are a chosen race, a royal priesthood, a holy nation, a people for his own possession, that you may proclaim the excellencies of him who called you out of darkness into his marvelous light." (1 Peter 2:9 ESV)

Paul called us "ambassadors" sent forth to plead with men to be reconciled with God through Jesus Christ.

And Paul wrote in Ephesians 3:20:

"Now to Him who is able to do far more abundantly than all that we ask or think, according to the **power** *at work within us, (Ephesians 3.20 ESV)*

Thus, we have Christ's power and that is His authority.

And let us make sure we see this: We are to…

Go with authority over evil.

When Christ is preached in our homes in family worship there is power over evil. When Christ is shared in love with others, there is life changing power that will restore marriage, give comfort in grieving, and translate a dead sinner into a living saint of God.

Now let us see not only the Commission, but there is more:

Genuine disciples, like the Twelve, are sent with a Command.

The command of Jesus involved how they should go. He allowed a staff, a walking stick. He allowed sandals. But He forbid bread, a bag for supplies, money and an extra tunic, which was used for a covering at night. In other words, they were to go and depend on Jesus alone for the journey.

This may very well be the central part of this that many of you need. It is certainly what pastors and church leaders need to hear. Jesus is not sending us with everything neat and tidy. Christ is calling us to go and He is showing us that if He calls, He will equip, and if He equips, He will sustain.

Often, I am called upon to teach in seminaries on church planting. The first two days are spent in going back to the pastoral Epistles because I want these pastoral students to become reacquainted with the call of God on their lives. I want them to see that I have no methods to offer them, no new thing to add to their calls and the gifts of God on their lives. We will just go line-by-line, verse-by-verse through 1 and 2 Timothy and Titus until we get it. Then we may talk about how to plant a church. But we need to trust in Jesus for church growth not in methods. We need to trust in Jesus if we are called to go to the mission field, not in whether or not we have all of the money that we need. God will provide if God has called and God has sent.

Now, He also tells them to just stay where they land. They are to go out from there, which means that they can go out and minister from there, but if someone will take them in, that is their home base, their staging area, if you will, for Gospel work. You don't have to worry about this. Have you ever heard, "Bloom where you are planted?" This is the biblical place to support such a saying. God will direct us and we stay there until He directs us elsewhere. If our message is rejected, then, according to Jesus, we go elsewhere.

There is a sense of dependence on Christ and a sense of urgency in the Gospel in all of this.

Now, finally, let us see about this "sending" that…

Faithful followers, like the Twelve, are sent with a Communiqué.

The message is this, according to verse 12: "repent." Matthew adds, "The kingdom of God has come." And Luke sums it up by saying, Preach the Gospel." What is the Gospel message? "Turn from your sins for in the coming of Jesus of Nazareth, the Kingdom of God has come to earth. He is here. This is the One. Look for no other. The Call is upon you to turn to Him and Him alone."

Verse 13 gives us the necessary companion to this first message: "Heal them." The oil mentioned is simply a sign. The olive oil could not produce the sort of instantaneous, miraculous healing that is under view here. These men had the supernatural touch of God, the power to heal and cast out demons. We do not have that power. We are not the Twelve. But we are to bring healing.

Indeed, it is here that we learn a vital truth: the Gospel must go forth in Word and in Deed. Not Word alone. Not Deed alone. One is intellectualism or fundamentalism in the worst sense and the other is a social Gospel and neither is the true Gospel. The Gospel goes forth in Deed as we feed the poor. And as we feed the poor and also share Jesus Christ with them, the Gospel goes forth in Word as well. The Gospel goes forth as we comfort the grieving. But it goes forth as we share the beauty of our Savior's grace as we minister physical and emotional comfort.

One of my former assistants telephoned me a few nights ago to tell me how God is blessing him. He went out and planted a church and now that it is established he has sought other ways to do the work of an evangelist. So he got involved with hospice. He told me that he was called in to be with a family of an aging and dying family member. As he met her, he held her hand, and with the sons and daughters and in-laws and grandchildren all hovered around her bed, he diagnosed her spiritual condition. He saw clearly that this woman was teetering on the edge of eternity without Christ. So, he told her the Gospel, that she was a sinner and in danger of soon standing before the judgment seat of Almighty God in her sins, but that Christ had come and died on a cross and if she repented she would be saved. The family said, "Pastor, you're a bit rough here." But the woman interrupted them and asked to pray to receive this One she had heard of all of her life. My former assistant then faithfully came into her room daily to teach her and sing with her. A few weeks ago, after work and a hard game of racquetball, he decided to drop by the nursing home before going to his house. The bed was empty. She was gone. A nurse came upon his astonishment and said, "Aren't you the one who came and sang hymns to her last night? "Yes," he said. "Well," the nurse smiled and spoke softly, "you sang her right into heaven."

We are called to be taught and we are taught to be sent. And we are sent to speak Christ and be Christ for a world in need.

Conclusion

The mission of our church is intended to reflect this very truth: to gather, and grow and send out strong disciples of Jesus Christ.

Once, several of our elders were working with me to seek God and to reflect these Biblical principles for our church mission. I had offered this as a statement summarizing our mission: "To gather and to grow." But one of my friends, and our elders, pressed me. "Mike, we can't just gather and grow. We gotta go! Christ called us to not only teach us, but also to share that teaching with a world in need! We can't forget sending!"

He was right, of course. And that is how we got to "gathering, and growing and sending."

For that is a true disciple: *Called to be taught and taught to be sent.*

This is truly a Journey of a Lifetime. You are not alone. Your destination is in sight. Your road is paved by The Lord Himself. Your provisions for the journey are supplied by God. Others have gone before. More will follow. Many will miss it. But by God's grace alone, you are now here.

There is only one thing to do:

Let the journey begin.

Resources for the Journey
Bibliography

New Reformation Study Bible: English Standard Version. 1st ed. Phillipsburg, NJ: P&R Pub. 2005.

Blanchard, J. Ultimate Questions. Evangelical Press, 1987.

_____ Why Believe the Bible? : Evangelical Press, 2004.

Bibles, C. *ESV Study Bible (Trutone, Brown/Cordovan, Portfolio Design)*. Crossway, 2009.

Boice, James Montgomery, and Philip Graham Ryken. *The Doctrines of Grace: Rediscovering the Evangelical Gospel*. Wheaton, Ill.: Crossway Books, 2002.

Boice, James Montgomery, and Benjamin E. Sasse. *Here We Stand: A Call from Confessing Evangelicals*. Grand Rapids, Mich.: Baker Books, 1996.

Bonhoeffer, D. *The Cost of Discipleship*. Touchstone, 2012.

Bridges, J., et al. *The Great Exchange: My Sin for His Righteousness*. Crossway, 2007. .

Chapell, Bryan. *Why Do We Baptize Infants?* : P & R Publishing, 2007. .

_____. *Holiness by Grace: Delighting in the Joy That Is Our Strength*. Wheaton, Ill.: Crossway Books, 2001.

Hallesby, Ole. *Prayer*. Minneapolis: Augsburg, 1994.

Johnson, Terry. *When Grace Comes Home: The Practical Difference That Calvinism Makes*. Christian Focus, 2003.

Kennedy, D. James, and Tom Stebbins. *Evangelism Explosion: Equipping Churches for Friendship, Evangelism, Discipleship, and Healthy Growth*. 4th ed. Wheaton, Ill.: Tyndale House Publishers, 1996.

Kistemaker, S.J. *Exposition of the Epistles of Peter and of the Epistle of Jude*. Baker, 1987.

Ladd, G.E. *The Gospel of the Kingdom: Scriptural Studies in the Kingdom of God*. Eerdmans, 1959.

Lewis, C. S. *The Case for Christianity*. 1st Collier Books ed. New York: Collier Books, 1989.

_____. *The Complete C.S. Lewis Signature Classics*. 1st ed. [San Francisco, Calif.]: HarperSanFrancisco, 2002.

_____. *Miracles: A Preliminary Study*. [San Francisco]: HarperSanFrancisco, 2001.

Lloyd-Jones, David Martyn. *The Plight of Man and the Power of God*. [2d ed. Grand Rapids, W.B. Eerdmans Pub. Co., 1966.

Machen, J.G. *Virgin Birth of Christ*. Lutterworth Press, 1987.

McDowell, J. *The New Evidence That Demands a Verdict*. T. Nelson, 1999.

Milton, Michael A. *Hit by Friendly Fire: What Do to When Fellow Believers Hurt You*. EVANGELICAL Press, 2011.

_____. *What God Starts God Completes Pb: Updated Third Edition*. Christian Focus Publications, 2012.

_____. *What Is Perseverance of the Saints?* Basics of the Reformed Faith. Phillipsburg, N.J.: P & R Pub., 2009.

_____. *What Is the Doctrine of Adoption?* Basics of the Reformed Faith: P&R Publishing, 2012.

Murray, John. Redemption, Accomplished and Applied. Grand Rapids,: W. B. Eerdmans Pub. Co., 1955.

Overman, D.L. A Case for the Divinity of Jesus: Examining the Earliest Evidence. Rowman & Littlefield Publishers, 2009.

Packer, J. I., and J. C. Ryle. Faithfulness and Holiness: The Witness of J.C. Ryle: An Appreciation by J.I. Packer. Wheaton, Ill.: Crossway Books, 2002.

_____ Knowing God. Hodder & Stoughton, 2011.

_____. Knowing God Study Guide. InterVarsity Press, 1993.

Phillips, R.D. What Is the Lord's Supper? : P & R Pub., 2005.

Pratt, R. Spirit of the Reformation Study Bible. Zondervan, 2003.

Ryken, P.G. When You Pray: Making the Lord's Prayer Your Own. P&R Pub., 2006.

Sproul, R. C. Knowing Scripture. Downers Grove, Ill.: Inter Varsity Press, 1977.

_____. Saved from What? Wheaton, Ill.: Crossway Books, 2002.

Stott, John R. W. *Basic Christianity*. 2nd ed. Leicester: Inter-Varsity, 2002.

_____. *The Cross of Christ*. 20th anniversary ed. Downers Grove, Ill.: IVP Books, 2006.

Strobel, L. *The Case for the Resurrection*. Zondervan, 2010.

Walter C. Kaiser, J. *The Messiah in the Old Testament*. Zondervan, 1995.

Warfield, Benjamin Breckinridge. *The Plan of Salvation*. 1st Simpson Pub. Co. re ed. Boonton, N. J.: Simpson Pub. Co., 1989.

Wright, C.J.H. *Salvation Belongs to Our God: Celebrating the Bible's Central Story*. InterVarsity Press, 2008.

Affirmation of Faith Resources

The Ten Commandments, Lord's Prayer, and the Apostles' Creed have long been the basic articles of the Christian faith which help us to begin our journey. They are not meant to be learned for meaningless repetition, but that doesn't mean that one should ignore the power of rote memory. Placing these truths in our minds as well as our hearts provides us with a rudimentary framework for the Christian faith. The Ten Commandments reminds us that God saved us to a new life of following Him. To follow Him through His revealed Word about our relationship with Himself, with the deep part of our own selves, and with others in community, brings blessings and life. The Ten Commandments do not save us. We are saved by God's grace through Jesus Christ. The Commandments guide us into a new life of following God. Likewise, the Lord's Prayer, as we have shown, is a guide to prayer. If we had nothing other than this guide, memorized and prayed, broken apart phrase by phrase, we would have all that we need to come to God according to His method of prayer for us. Finally, the Apostles' Creed is an ancient summary of what the Bible teaches about the very basics of our faith. Those basics unite us with other believers all through time and all around the world. So do memorize these, but memorize them to activate them into living expressions of your heart and life in the community of God's people, the Church.

I have added a summary of the teaching of the Holy Scripture as summarized by the Westminster Shorter Catechism adapted for children. The Westminster Catechism was adopted by the English, Welsh, and Scottish Puritans during the ascendancy of the Puritans in Great Britain. The document has long been considered a high mark in confessional Christianity. This particular summary has been created over the years for children of Reformed and Presbyterian churches, but has been increasingly used by Christians of many other fellowships. I pray it will be of help to you as you begin your journey of following Christ.

The Ten Commandments

(Taken from the Anglican *Book of Common Prayer*, 1928, with the liturgical responses and the catechetical or teaching notes remaining)
God spake these words, and said:

I am the Lord thy God who brought thee out of the land of Egypt, out of the house of bondage. Thou shalt have none other gods but me.
Lord have mercy upon us, and incline our hearts to keep this law.

Thou shalt not make to thyself any graven image, nor the likeness of any thing that is in heaven above, or in the earth beneath, or in the water under the earth; thou shalt not bow down to them, nor worship them.
Lord have mercy upon us, and incline our hearts to keep this law.

Thou shalt not take the Name of the Lord thy God in vain.
Lord have mercy upon us, and incline our hearts to keep this law.

Remember that thou keep holy the Sabbath day.
Lord have mercy upon us, and incline our hearts to keep this law.

Honor thy father and thy mother.
Lord have mercy upon us, and incline our hearts to keep this law.

Thou shalt do no murder.
Lord have mercy upon us, and incline our hearts to keep this law.

Thou shalt not commit adultery.
Lord have mercy upon us, and incline our hearts to keep this law.

Thou shalt not steal.
Lord have mercy upon us, and incline our hearts to keep this law.

Thou shalt not bear false witness against thy neighbor.
Lord have mercy upon us, and incline our hearts to keep this law.

Thou shalt not covet.
Lord have mercy upon us, and write all these thy laws in our hearts, we beseech thee.

Q. 1. *What are the Ten Commandments?*
A. The Ten Commandments are the laws given to Moses and the people of Israel.

Q. 2. *What do we learn from these commandments?*
A. We learn two things: our duty to God, and our duty to our neighbors.

Q. 3. *What is our duty to God?*
A. Our duty is to believe and trust in God;

    I   To love and obey God and to bring others to know him;

    II   To put nothing in the place of God;

    III   To show God respect in thought, word, and deed;

    IV   And to set aside regular times for worship, prayer, and the study of God's ways.

Q. 4. *What is our duty to our neighbors?*
A. Our duty to our neighbors is to love them as ourselves, and to do to other people as we wish them to do to us;

    V   To love, honor, and help our parents and family; to honor those in authority, and to meet their just demands;

    VI   To show respect for the life God has given us; to work and pray for peace; to bear no malice, prejudice, or hatred in our hearts; and to be kind to all the creatures of God;

    VII   To use our bodily desires as God intended;

    VIII   To be honest and fair in our dealings; to seek justice, freedom, and the necessities of life for all people; and to use our talents and possessions as ones who must answer for them to God;

    IX   To speak the truth, and not to mislead others by our silence;

    X   To resist temptations to envy, greed, and jealousy; to rejoice in other people's gifts and graces; and to do our duty for the love of God, Who has called us into fellowship with him.

Q. 5. *What is the purpose of the Ten Commandments?*
A.   The Ten Commandments were given to define our relationship with God and our neighbors.

Q. 6. *Since we do not fully obey them, are they useful at all?*
A.   Since we do not fully obey them, we see more clearly our sin and our need for redemption.

The Lord's Prayer (Traditional)

Our Father, which art in heaven,
Hallowed be thy Name.
Thy Kingdom come.
Thy will be done in earth,
As it is in heaven.
Give us this day our daily bread.
And forgive us our trespasses,
As we forgive them that trespass against us.
And lead us not into temptation,
But deliver us from evil.
For thine is the kingdom,
The power, and the glory,
For ever and ever.
Amen.
(Taken from the *Anglican Book of Common Prayer*, 1662).

The Apostles' Creed (a Contemporary Version)

I believe in God, the Father Almighty,
  Creator of heaven and earth;
I believe in Jesus Christ, his only Son, our Lord.
  He was conceived by the power of the Holy Spirit
    and born of the Virgin Mary.
  He suffered under Pontius Pilate,
    Was crucified, died, and was buried.
  He descended to the dead.
  On the third day he rose again.
  He ascended into heaven,

and is seated at the right hand of the Father.

He will come again to judge the living and the dead.
I believe in the Holy Spirit,
    the holy catholic Church,
    the communion of saints,
    the forgiveness of sins
    the resurrection of the body,
    and the life everlasting. Amen.

The Westminster Catechism for Children
An Introduction to the Shorter Catechism

Q. 1. Who made you?
A. God.

Q. 2. What else did God make?
A. God made all things.

Q. 3. Why did God make you and all things ?
A. For his own glory.

Q. 4. How can you glorify God?
A. By loving him and doing what he commands.

Q. 5. Why ought you to glorify God?
A. Because he made me and takes care of me.

Q. 6. Are there more gods than one?
A. There is only one God.

Q. 7. In how many persons does this one God exist?
A. In three persons.

Q. 8. What are they?
A. The Father, the Son, and the Holy Ghost.

Q. 9. What is God?
A. God is a Spirit, and has not a body like men.

Q. 10. Where is God?
A. God is everywhere.

Q. 11. Can you see God?
A. No; I cannot see God, but he always sees me.

Q. 12. Does God know all things?
A. Yes; nothing can be hid from God.

Q. 13. Can God do all things?
A. Yes; God can do all his holy will.

Q. 14. Where do you learn how to love and obey God?
A. In the Bible alone.

Q. 15. Who wrote the Bible?
A. Holy men who were taught by the Holy Spirit.

Q. 16. Who were our first parents?
A. Adam and Eve.

Q. 17. Of what were our first parents made?
A. God made the body of Adam out of the ground, and formed Eve from the body of Adam.

Q. 18. What did God give Adam and Eve besides bodies?
A. He gave them souls that could never die.

Q. 19. Have you a soul as well as a body?
A. Yes; I have a soul that can never die.

Q. 20. How do you know that you have a soul?
A. Because the Bible tells me so.

Q. 21. In what condition did God make Adam and Eve?
A. He made them holy and happy.

Q. 22. What is a covenant?
A. An agreement between two or more persons.

Q. 23. What covenant did God make with Adam?
A. The covenant of works.

Q. 24. What was Adam bound to do by the covenant of works?
A. To obey God perfectly.

Q. 25. What did God promise in the covenant of works?
A. To reward Adam with life if he obeyed him.

Q. 26. What did God threaten in the covenant of works?
A. To punish Adam with death if he disobeyed.

Q. 27. Did Adam keep the covenant of works?
A. No; he sinned against God.

Q. 28. What is Sin?
A. Sin is any want of conformity unto, or transgression of the law of God.

Q. 29. What is meant by want of conformity?
A. Not being or doing what God requires.

Q. 30. What is meant by transgression?
A. Doing what God forbids.

Q. 31. What was the sin of our first parents?
A. Eating the forbidden fruit.

Q. 32. Who tempted them to this sin?
A. The devil tempted Eve, and she gave the fruit to Adam.

Q. 33. What befell our first parents when they had sinned?
A. Instead of being holy and happy, they became sinful and miserable.

Q. 34. Did Adam act for himself alone in the covenant of works?
A. No; he represented all his posterity.

Q. 35. What effect had the sin of Adam on all mankind?
A. All mankind are born in a state of sin and misery.

Q. 36. What is that sinful nature which we inherit from Adam called?
A. Original sin.

Q. 37. What does every sin deserve?
A. The wrath and curse of God.

Q. 38. Can any one go to heaven with this sinful nature?
A. No; our hearts must be changed before we can be fit for heaven.

Q. 39. What is a change of heart called?
A. Regeneration.

Q. 40. Who can change a sinner's heart?
A. The Holy Spirit alone.

Q. 41. Can any one be saved through the covenant of works?
A. None can be saved through the covenant of works.

Q. 42. Why can none be saved through the covenant of works?
A. Because all have broken it, and are condemned by it

Q. 43. With whom did God the Father make the covenant of grace?
A. With Christ, his eternal Son.

Q. 44. Whom did Christ represent in the covenant of grace?
A. His elect people.

Q. 45. What did Christ undertake in the covenant of grace?
A. To keep the whole law for his people, and to suffer the punishment due to their sins.

Q. 46. Did our Lord Jesus Christ ever commit the least sin?
A. No; he was holy, harmless, and undefiled.

Q. 47. How could the Son of God suffer?
A. Christ, the Son of God, became man that he might obey and suffer in our nature.

Q. 48. What is meant by the Atonement?
A. Christ's satisfying divine justice, by his sufferings and death, in the place of sinners.

Q. 49. What did God the Father undertake in the covenant of grace?
A. To justify and sanctify those for whom Christ should die.

Q. 50. What is justification?
A. It is God's forgiving sinners, and treating them as if they had never sinned.

Q. 51. What is sanctification?
A. It is God's making sinners holy in heart and conduct.

Q. 52. For whom did Christ obey and suffer?
A. For those whom the Father had given him.

Q. 53. What kind of life did Christ live on earth?
A. A life of poverty and suffering.

Q. 54. What kind of death did Christ die?
A. The painful and shameful death of the cross.

Q. 55. Who will be saved?
A. Only those who repent of sin, believe in Christ, and lead holy lives.

Q. 56. What is it to repent?
A. To be sorry for sin, and to hate and forsake it because it is displeasing to God.

Q. 57. What is it to believe or have faith in Christ?
A. To trust in Christ alone for salvation.

Q. 58. Can you repent and believe in Christ by your own power?
A. No; I can do nothing good without the help of God's Holy Spirit.

Q. 59. How can you get the help of the Holy Spirit?
A. God has told us that we must pray to him for the Holy Spirit.

Q. 60. How long ago is it since Christ died?
A. More than nineteen hundred years.

Q. 61. How were pious persons saved before the coming of Christ?
A. By believing in a Savior to come.

Q. 62. How did they show their faith?
A. By offering sacrifices on God's altar.

Q. 63. What did these sacrifices represent?
A. Christ, the Lamb of God, who was to die for sinners.

Q. 64. What offices has Christ?
A. Christ has three offices.

Q. 65. What are they?
A. The offices of a prophet, of a priest, and of a king.

Q. 66. How is Christ a prophet?
A. Because he teaches us the will of God.

Q. 67. How is Christ a priest?
A. Because he died for our sins and pleads with God for us.

Q. 68. How is Christ a king?
A. Because he rules over us and defends us.

Q. 69. Why do you need Christ as a prophet?
A. Because I am ignorant.

Q. 70. Why do you need Christ as a priest?
A. Because I am guilty.

Q. 71. Why do you need Christ as a king?
A. Because I am weak and helpless.

Q. 72. How many commandments did God give on Mount Sinai?
A. Ten commandments.

Q. 73. What are the ten commandments sometimes called?
A. The Decalogue.

Q. 74. What do the first four commandments teach?
A. Our duty to God.

Q. 75. What do the last six commandments teach?
A. Our duty to our fellow men.

Q. 76. What is the sum of the ten commandments?
A. To love God with all my heart, and my neighbor as myself.

Q. 77. Who is your neighbor?
A. All my fellow men are my neighbors.

Q. 78. Is God pleased with those who love and obey him?
A. Yes; he says, "I love them that love me."

Q. 79. Is God displeased with those who do not love and obey him?
A. Yes; "God is angry with the wicked every day."

Q. 80. What is the first commandment?
A. The first commandment is, Thou shalt have no other gods before me.

Q. 81. What does the first commandment teach us?
A. To worship God alone.

Q. 82. What is the second commandment?
A. The second commandment is, Thou shalt not make unto thee any graven image, or any likeness of any things that is in heaven above, or that is in the earth beneath, or that is in the water under the earth; thou shalt not bow down thyself to them, nor serve them: for I, the Lord thy God, am a jealous God, visiting the iniquity of the fathers upon the children unto the third and fourth generation of them that hate me; and showing mercy unto thousands of them that love me, and keep my commandments.

Q. 83. What does the second commandment teach us?
A. To worship God in a proper manner, and to avoid idolatry.

Q. 84. What is the third commandment?
A. The third commandment is, Thou shalt not take the name of the Lord thy God in vain: for the Lord will not hold him guiltless that taketh his name in vain.

Q. 85. What does the third commandment teach me?
A. To reverence God's name, word, and works.

Q. 86. What is the fourth commandment?
A. The fourth commandment is, Remember the Sabbath day to keep it holy. Six days shalt thou labor, and do all thy work, but the seventh day is the Sabbath of the Lord thy God; in it thou shalt not do any work, thou, nor thy son, nor thy daughter, nor thy manservant, nor thy maidservant, nor thy cattle, nor thy stranger that is within thy gates: for in six days the Lord made heaven and earth, the sea, and all that in them is, and rested the

seventh day; wherefore the Lord blessed the Sabbath Day, and hallowed it.

Q. 87. What does the fourth commandment teach us?
A. To keep the Sabbath holy.

Q. 88. What day of the week is the Christian Sabbath?
A. The first day of the week, called the Lord's day.

Q. 89. Why is it called the Lord's day?
A. Because on that day Christ rose from the dead.

Q. 90. How should the Sabbath be spent?
A. In prayer and praise, in hearing and reading God's Word, and in doing good to our fellow men.

Q. 91. What is the fifth commandment?
A. The fifth commandment is, Honor thy father and thy mother, that thy days may be long upon the land which the Lord thy God giveth thee.

Q. 92. What does the fifth commandment teach me?
A. To love and obey our parents and teachers.

Q. 93. What is the sixth commandment?
A. The sixth commandment is, Thou shalt not kill.

Q. 94. What does the sixth commandment teach us?
A. To avoid angry passions.

Q. 95. What is the seventh commandment?
A. The seventh commandment is, Thou shalt not commit adultery.

Q. 96. What does the seventh commandment teach us?
A   To be pure in heart, language, and conduct.

Q. 97. What is the eighth commandment?
A. The eighth commandment is, Thou shalt not steal.

Q. 98. What does the eighth commandment teach us?
A. To be honest and industrious.

Q. 99. What is the ninth commandment?
A. The ninth commandment is, Thou shalt not bear false witness against thy neighbor.

Q. 100. What does the ninth commandment teach us?
A. To tell the truth.

Q. 101. What is the tenth commandment?
A. The tenth commandment is, Thou shalt not covet thy neighbor's house, thou shalt not covet thy neighbor's wife, nor his man servant, nor his maidservant, nor his ox, nor his ass, nor any thing that is thy neighbor's.

Q. 102. What does the tenth commandment teach us?
A. To be content with our lot.

Q. 103. Can any man keep these ten commandments perfectly?
A. No mere man, since the fall of Adam, ever did or can keep the ten commandments perfectly.

Q. 104. Of what use are the ten commandments to us?
A. They teach us our duty, and show our need of a Savior.

Q. 105. What is prayer?
A. Prayer is asking God for things which he has promised to give.

Q. 106. In whose name should we pray?
A. Only in the name of Christ.

Q. 107. What has Christ given us to teach us how to pray?
A. The Lord's Prayer.

Q. 108. Repeat the Lord's Prayer.
A. Our Father which art in heaven, Hallowed be thy name. Thy kingdom come. Thy will be done in earth, as it is in heaven. Give us this day our daily bread. And forgive us our debts, as we forgive our debtors. And lead us not into temptation, but deliver us from evil: For thine is the kingdom, and the power, and the glory, for ever. Amen.

Q. 109. How many petitions are there in The Lord's Prayer?
A. Six.

Q. 110. What is the first petition?
A. "Hallowed be thy name."

Q. 111. What do we pray for in the first petition?
A. That God's name may be honored by us and all men.

Q. 112. What is the second petition?
A. "Thy kingdom come."

Q. 113. What do we pray for in the second petition?
A. That the gospel may be preached in all the world, and believed and obeyed by us and all men.

Q. 114. What is the third petition?
A. "Thy will be done in earth, as it is in heaven."

Q. 115. What do we pray for in the third petition?
A. That men on earth may serve God as the angels do in heaven.

Q. 116. What is the fourth petition?
A. "Give us this day our daily bread."

Q. 117. What do we pray for in the fourth petition?
A. That God would give us all things needful for our bodies and souls.

Q. 118. What is the fifth petition?
A. "And forgive us our debts, as we forgive our debtors."

Q. 119. What do we pray for in the fifth petition?
A. That God would pardon our sins for Christ's sake, and enable us to forgive those who have injured us.

Q. 120. What is the sixth petition?
A. "And lead us not into temptation, but deliver us from evil."

Q. 121. What do we pray for in the sixth petition?
A. That God would keep us from sin.

Q. 122. How many sacraments are there?
A. Two.

Q. 123. What are they?
A. Baptism and the Lord's Supper.

Q. 124. Who appointed these sacraments?
A. The Lord Jesus Christ.

Q. 125. Why did Christ appoint these sacraments?
A. To distinguish his disciples from the world, and to comfort and strengthen them.

Q. 126. What sign is used in baptism?
A. The washing with water.

Q. 127. What does this signify?
A. That we are cleansed from sin by the blood of Christ.

Q. 128. In whose name are we baptized?
A. In the name of the Father, and of the Son, and of the Holy Ghost.

Q. 129. Who are to be baptized?
A. Believers and their children.

Q. 130. Why should infants be baptized?
A. Because they have a sinful nature and need a Savior.

Q. 131. Does Christ care for little children?
A. Yes; for he says, "Suffer the little children to come unto me, and forbid them not: for of such is the kingdom of God."

Q. 132. To what does your baptism bind you?
A. To be a true follower of Christ.

Q. 133. What is the Lord's Supper?
A. The eating of bread and drinking of wine in remembrance of the sufferings and death of Christ.

Q. 134. What does the bread represent?
A. The body of Christ, broken for our sins.

Q. 135. What does the wine represent?
A. The blood of Christ, shed for our salvation.

Q. 136. Who should partake of the Lord's Supper?
A. Only those who repent of their sins, believe in Christ for salvation, and love their fellow men.

Q. 137. Did Christ remain in the tomb after his crucifixion?
A. No; he rose from the tomb on the third day after his death.

Q. 138. Where is Christ now?
A. In heaven, interceding for sinners.

Q. 139. Will he come again?
A. Yes; at the last day Christ will come to judge the world.

Q. 140. What becomes of men at death?
A. The body returns to dust, and the soul goes into the world of spirits.

Q. 141. Will the bodies of the dead be raised to life again?
A. Yes; "The trumpet shall sound, and the dead shall be raised."

Q. 142. What will become of the wicked in the day of judgment?
A. They shall be cast into hell.

Q. 143. What is hell?
A. A place of dreadful and endless torment.

Q. 144. What will become of the righteous?
A. They shall be taken to heaven.

Q. 145. What is heaven?
A. A glorious and happy place, where the righteous shall be forever with the Lord.

Endnotes

1. "For everyone who calls on the name of the Lord will be saved" (Romans 10:13 ESV).

2. James Montgomery Boice and Benjamin E. Sasse, *Here We Stand: A Call from Confessing Evangelicals* (Grand Rapids, Mich.: Baker Books, 1996).

3. "For the wages of sin is death, but the free gift of God is eternal life in Christ Jesus our Lord" (Romans 6:23 ESV).

4. "For by grace you have been saved through faith. And this is not your own doing; it is the gift of God, not a result of works, so that no one may boast" (Ephesians 2:8-9 ESV).

5. David Martyn Lloyd-Jones, *The Plight of Man and the Power of God*, [2d ed. (Grand Rapids,: W.B. Eerdmans Pub. Co., 1966). See also R. C. Sproul, *Saved from What?* (Wheaton, Ill.: Crossway Books, 2002).

6. See J. Murray, *The Imputation of Adam's Sin* (Presbyterian and Reformed, 1959). See also John Murray, Redemption, Accomplished and Applied (Grand Rapids,: W. B. Eerdmans Pub. Co., 1955).

7. See J. Bridges, B. Bevington, S. Ferguson and S.B. Ferguson, *The Great Exchange: My Sin for His* Righteousness (Crossway, 2007).

8. "The Son of God, the second Person in the Trinity, being very and eternal God, of one substance, and equal with the Father, did, when the fullness of time was come, take upon him man's nature, with all the essential properties and common infirmities thereof; yet without sin: being conceived by the power of the Holy Ghost, in the womb of the Virgin Mary, of her substance. So that two whole, perfect, and distinct natures, the Godhead and the manhood, were inseparably joined together in one person, without conversion, composition, or confusion. Which person is very God and very man, yet one Christ, the only Mediator between God and man." See The Westminster Confession of Faith, Chapter Three, article two, at Reformed.com (http://www.reformed.org/documents/index.html?mainframe=http://www.reformed.org/documents/westminster_conf_of_faith.html), accessed on September 4, 2012. For a review of six major Protestant confessions of faith and a study on the doctrine of Christ and other essential Christian teachings, we commend R. Pratt, *Spirit of the Reformation Study Bible* (Zondervan, 2003).

9. "In the beginning was the Word, and the Word was with God, and the Word was God... And the Word was made flesh, and dwelt among us, (and we beheld his glory, the glory as of the only begotten of the Father,) full of grace and truth," John 1:1, 14 KJV); "I and my Father are one." (John 10:30 KJV); "And when he saw their faith, he said unto him, Man, thy sins are forgiven thee. And the scribes and the Pharisees began to reason, saying, Who is this which speaketh blasphemies? Who can forgive sins, but God alone? But when Jesus perceived their thoughts, he answering said unto them, What reason ye in your hearts? Whether is easier, to say, Thy sins be forgiven thee; or to say, Rise up and walk? But that ye may know that the Son of man hath power upon earth to forgive sins, (he said unto the sick of the palsy,) I say unto thee, Arise, and take up thy couch, and go into thine house." (Luke 5:20-24 KJV)

10. C. S. Lewis, *The Case for Christianity*, 1st Collier Books ed. (New York: Collier Books, 1989). See also L. Strobel, *The Case for the Resurrection* (Zondervan, 2010). J. McDowell, *The New Evidence That Demands a Verdict* (T. Nelson, 1999).

11. "I and the Father are one" (John 10:30 ESV). For a scholarly review of the self identity of Jesus of Nazareth as God in the Bible see D.L. Overman, *A Case for the Divinity of Jesus: Examining the Earliest Evidence* (Rowman & Littlefield Publishers, 2009).

12. "For in him the whole fullness of deity dwells bodily" (Colossians 2:9 ESV).

13. J.G. Machen, *Virgin Birth of Christ* (Lutterworth Press, 1987).

14 C. S. Lewis, *Miracles: A Preliminary Study* ([San Francisco]: HarperSanFrancisco, 2001).

15 See Overman, *A Case for the Divinity of Jesus: Examining the Earliest Evidence*.

16 Simon Peter replied, "You are the Christ, the Son of the living God." (Matthew 16:16 ESV)

17 We commend the Commentary on 2 Peter by Dr. Simon Kistemaker: S.J. Kistemaker, *Exposition of the Epistles of Peter and of the Epistle of Jude* (Baker, 1987).

18 John R. W. Stott, Basic Christianity, 2nd ed. (Leicester: Inter-Varsity, 2002).

19 D. James Kennedy and Tom Stebbins, *Evangelism Explosion : Equipping Churches for Friendship, Evangelism, Discipleship, and Healthy Growth*, 4th ed. (Wheaton, Ill.: Tyndale House Publishers, 1996).

20 John R. W. Stott, *The Cross of Christ*, 20th anniversary ed. (Downers Grove, Ill.: IVP Books, 2006).

21 Benjamin Breckinridge Warfield, *The Plan of Salvation*, 1st Simpson Pub. Co. re ed. (Boonton, N. J.: Simpson Pub. Co., 1989).

22 The Kingdom of God is the rule and reign of our Lord and Savior Jesus Christ. His rule, His Kingdom, is here, is growing, from the inside out, and will one day burst forth in cataclysmic form when He returns in visible, bodily form. See D. Bonhoeffer, *The Cost of Discipleship* (Touchstone, 2012) 166. See also G.E. Ladd, *The Gospel of the Kingdom: Scriptural Studies in the Kingdom of* God (Eerdmans, 1959).

23 "Then the seventh angel blew his trumpet, and there were loud voices in heaven, saying, "The kingdom of the world has become the kingdom of our Lord and of his Christ, and he shall reign forever and ever" (Revelation 11:15 ESV).

24 J.I. Packer, *Knowing God Study Guide* (InterVarsity Press, 1993) 22ff.

25 T. Johnson, *When Grace Comes Home: The Practical Difference That Calvinism Makes* (Christian Focus, 2003).

26 J.I. Packer, Knowing God (Hodder & Stoughton, 2011).

27 Bryan Chapell, *Holiness by Grace : Delighting in the Joy That Is Our Strength* (Wheaton, Ill.: Crossway Books, 2001).

28 R. C. Sproul, Knowing Scripture (Downers Grove, Ill.: Inter Varsity Press, 1977).

29 James Montgomery Boice and Philip Graham Ryken, *The Doctrines of Grace : Rediscovering the Evangelical Gospel* (Wheaton, Ill.: Crossway Books, 2002).

30 See "What the Old Testament Prophesied About the Messiah" (http://www.christianity.com/Christian%20Foundations/Jesus/11541169/0, accessed September 4, 2012. See also J. Walter C. Kaiser, *The Messiah in the Old Testament* (Zondervan, 1995).

31 Michael Anthony Milton, *What Is the Doctrine of Adoption?*, Basics of the Reformed Faith (P&R Publishing, 2012).

32 Michael A. Milton, *What Is Perseverance of the Saints?*, Basics of the Reformed Faith. (Phillipsburg, N.J.: P & R Pub., 2009).

33 We commend C. Bibles, *ESV Study Bible* (Crossway, 2009). We also commend *New Reformation Study Bible : English Standard Version*, 1st ed. (Phillipsburg, NJ: P&R Pub., 2005).

34 C.J.H. Wright, *Salvation Belongs to Our God: Celebrating the Bible's Central Story* (InterVarsity Press, 2008) 125.

35 B. Chapell, *Why Do We Baptize Infants?* (P & R Publishing, 2007).

36 R.D. Phillips, *What Is the Lord's Supper?* (P & R Pub., 2005).

37 Ole Hallesby, *Prayer* (Minneapolis: Augsburg, 1994).

38 Hallesby, *Prayer* 13.

39 P.G. Ryken, *When You Pray: Making the Lord's Prayer Your Own* (P&R Pub., 2006).

40 M. Milton, *What God Starts God Completes Pb: Updated Third Edition* (Christian Focus Publications, 2012).

41 Dietrich Bonhoeffer, *Writings Selected with an Introduction by Robert Coles*, "Modern Spiritual Masters Series" (Maryknoll, NY: Orbis Books, 2001), 43-44.

www.ingramcontent.com/pod-product-compliance
Lightning Source LLC
Chambersburg PA
CBHW061343040426
42444CB00011B/3064